We dress up

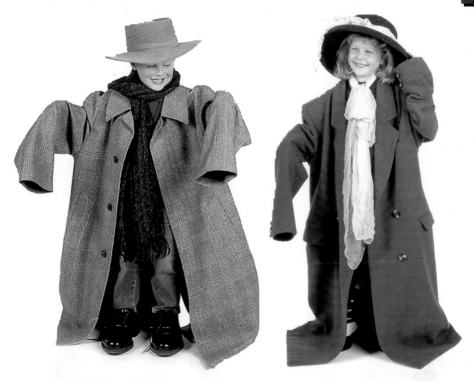

I am Dad.

Here is my coat.

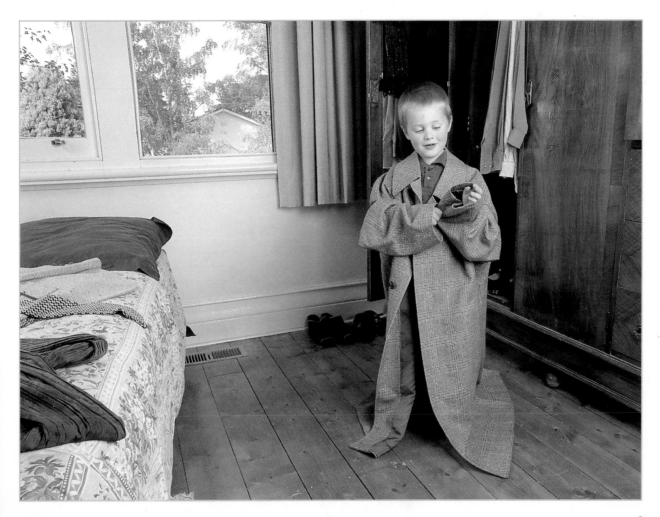

3

I am Mom.

Here is my coat.

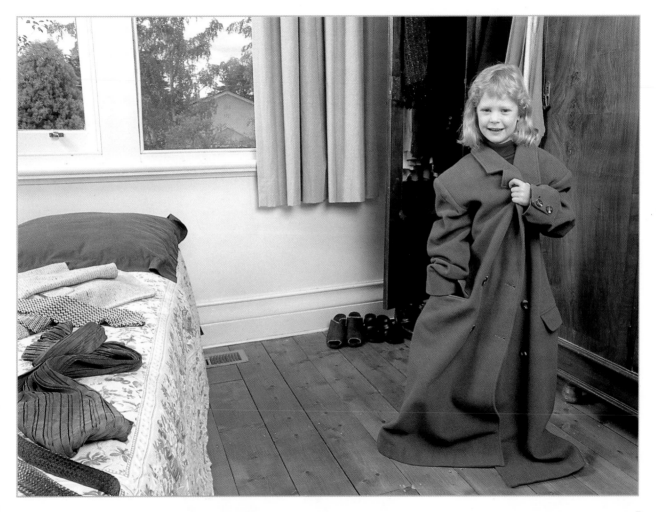

I am Dad.

Here is my hat.

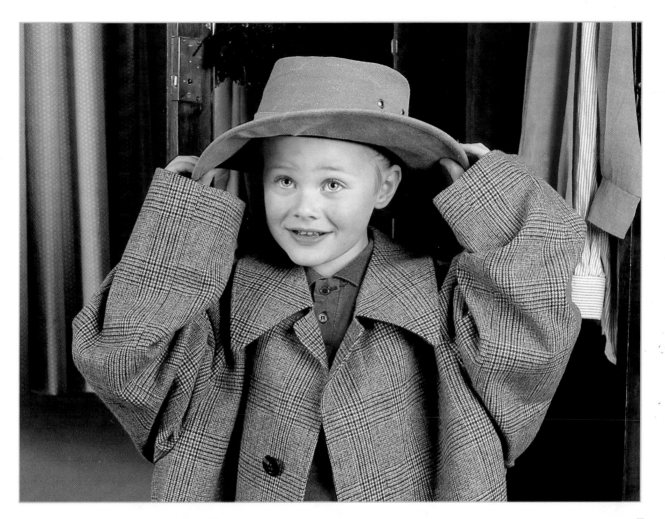

I am Mom.

Here is my hat.

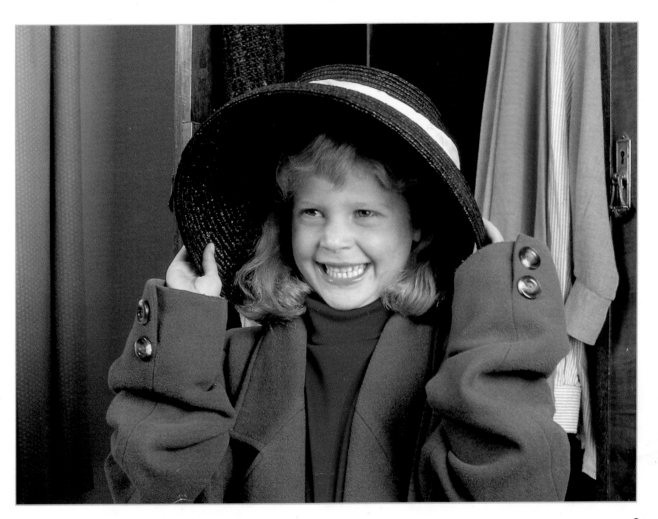

I am Dad.

Here is my scarf.

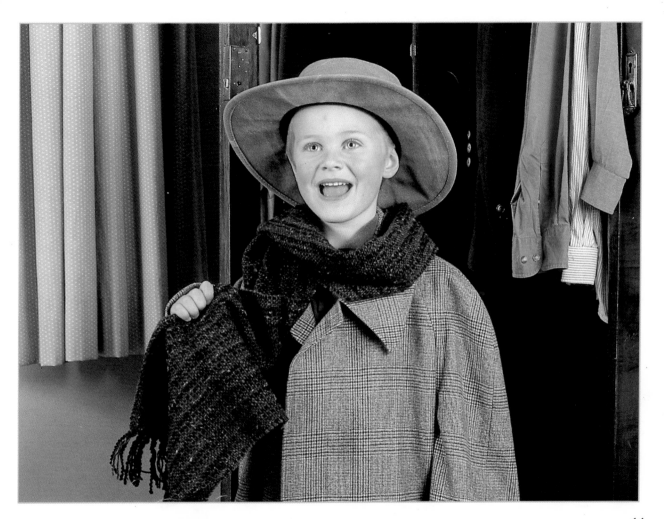

I am Mom.

Here is my scarf.

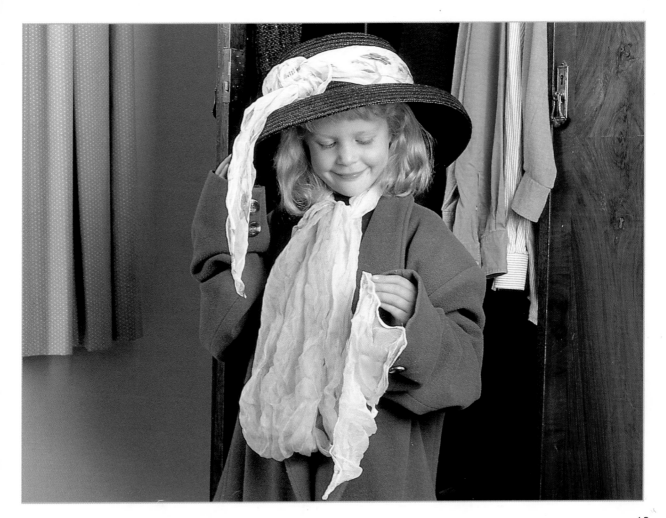

13

I am Dad.

Here are my shoes.

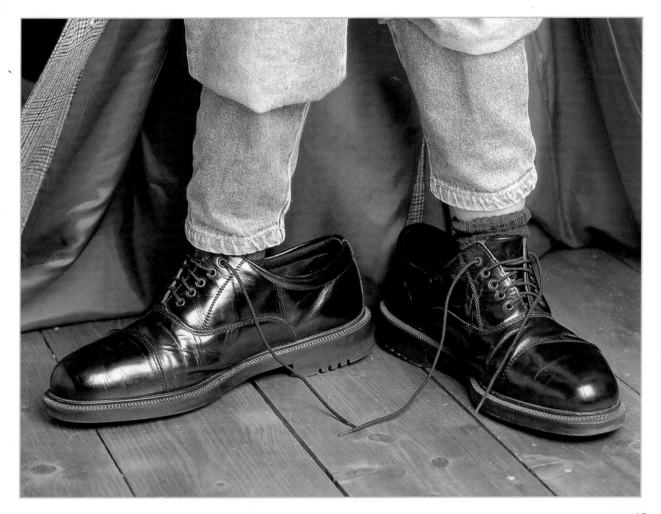

I am Mom.

Here are my shoes.

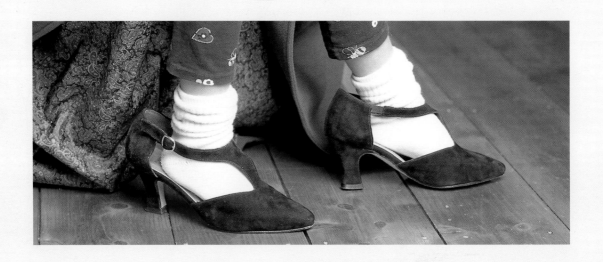